ECV193-Primary Sources of Colonial America (eBooks)

Cavendish Square 6 Volumes Flipbook
Set Price: $307.98
Reading Level: 6th Grade
Interest Level: Middle, Secondary
Accelerated Reader: No

Through primary sources of the time that documented the many reasons people left their homes in Europe and settled in the American colonies, this series provides insights to the waves of immigrants who headed for the New World and the contributions they made to the formation of a diverse nation. Readers will see the big moments at the dawning of the United States and its experiment in self-government through the eyes of the people who lived it. This lends perspective and insights to the ideals on which the United States was founded.

Title	Code	List Price	Our Price	Copyright	Prg
Colonial Interactions with Native Americans	ECV631350	$68.44	$51.33	2018	
From New Amsterdam to New York: Dutch Settlement of America	ECV631374	$68.44	$51.33	2018	
Jamestown and the Settlement of Virginia	ECV631398	$68.44	$51.33	2018	
Plymouth and the Settlement of New England	ECV631411	$68.44	$51.33	2018	
Slavery in Colonial America	ECV631435	$68.44	$51.33	2018	
The French and Indian War	ECV631459	$68.44	$51.33	2018	

Primary Sources of Colonial America

From New Amsterdam to New York: Dutch Settlement of America

Kate Shoup

Cavendish Square

New York

Published in 2018 by Cavendish Square Publishing, LLC
243 5th Avenue, Suite 136, New York, NY 10016

Library of Congress Cataloging-in-Publication Data

Names: Shoup, Kate, 1972- author.
Title: From New Amsterdam to New York : Dutch settlement of America / Kate Shoup.
Other titles: Dutch settlement of America
Description: New York : Cavendish Square Publishing, [2018] | Series: Primary sources of Colonial America | Includes bibliographical references and index.
Identifiers: LCCN 2017016270 (print) | LCCN 2017016715 (ebook) | ISBN 9781502631367 (library bound) | ISBN 9781502634580 (pbk.) | ISBN 9781502631374 (E-book)
Subjects: LCSH: Dutch--America--History--Juvenile literature. | Netherlands--Colonies--America--History--Juvenile literature. | New Netherland--History--Juvenile literature. | Frontier and pioneer life--New Netherland--Juvenile literature. | Netherlands--Commerce--America--History--Juvenile literature. | America--Commerce--Netherlands--History--Juvenile literature.
Classification: LCC E184.D9 (ebook) | LCC E184.D9 S48 2018 (print) | DDC 949.2/01--dc23
LC record available at https://lccn.loc.gov/2017016270

Editorial Director: David McNamara
Editor: Fletcher Doyle
Copy Editor: Rebecca Rohan
Associate Art Director: Amy Greenan
Designer: Lindsey Auten
Production Coordinator: Karol Szymczuk
Photo Research: J8 Media

Printed in the United States of America

CONTENTS

Forgotten Influence

V irtually every student in the United States studies the colonization of America. They're taught that the first English settlers landed in Virginia in 1607. They learn that this first group was followed by the Pilgrims, who founded the Plymouth colony in 1620. Over the next 125 years, they're told, more colonies formed—thirteen in all. Finally, they learn that in 1776, the residents of these thirteen colonies—fed up with English rule—linked arms in revolt. The result was the formation of the United States of America.

So the story goes, anyway.

In fact, from 1609 until 1664, much of this land belonged to another group of Europeans: the Dutch. This Dutch colony, called New Netherland, encompassed four of the original thirteen British colonies—New York, New Jersey, Delaware, and Connecticut—and supported outposts in Pennsylvania and Rhode Island.

For many years, little was known about New Netherland. It was believed that the Dutch kept meager records—and

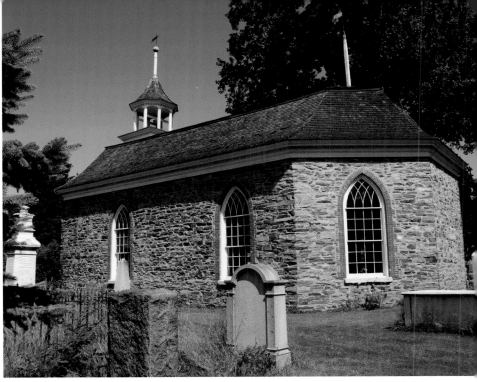

The Old Dutch Church of Sleepy Hollow dates to 1685. It is a reminder of the influence of the Dutch in the region and of New York's history of religious liberty.

that those they did keep did not survive. That's changing, however. Recently, historians discovered troves of documents that reveal the workings of this colony—its society, its culture, its practices, and perhaps most importantly, its people. These documents also reveal just how much of an impact New Netherland had on America—an impact that, until now, has gone largely unappreciated.

New Netherland, we now know, was a remarkably free society—a hallmark of modern American culture. This free society reflected the greater Dutch culture during this period—described by one historian as "the most progressive and culturally diverse society in Europe." Also, the Dutch believed in religious tolerance. The US Constitution guarantees that "Congress shall make no law respecting an establishment of religion, or prohibiting the free exercise thereof." Likewise, the Union of Utrecht, the Dutch nation's

The Dutch were the first Europeans to settle the area we now call New York. Here, Peter Stuyvesant lectures people on morality.

founding document, stated that "everyone shall remain free in religion and that no one may be persecuted or investigated because of religion." Unlike other European countries, which often closed their doors to outsiders, the Dutch accepted

From New Amsterdam to New York:
Dutch Settlement of America

everyone—Protestant, Catholic, Jew, Muslim, and otherwise. The result was a vibrant population and society.

While the English Pilgrims and Puritans colonized New England so they could practice their religion as they saw fit, the Dutch had another aim: to exploit the area's rich natural resources for profit. To achieve this, the country's powerful merchant class dangled the prospect of upward mobility to anyone willing to make the trip to the New World. People of all kinds accepted the challenge. The result was a very different kind of colony from those in New England. It was closer to the colony in Virginia, but it opened opportunity for more people than in Jamestown. Instead of the "prim, theocratic monoculture of the Pilgrim and Puritan colonies of New England," notes journalist Andrea Stone, New Netherland was a "cacophony of religions, races, and ethnic groups" as well as people involved in illegal activities such as smuggling and piracy.

Ultimately, New Netherland would not survive. In 1664, the English seized the region. However, its legacy of diversity and tolerance lives on in our modern United States.

CHAPTER ONE

Settlement of a New World

I n 1602, the Dutch government sponsored the formation of a new company, called the Vereenigde Oost-Indische Compagnie (Dutch East India Company) to participate in the Asian **spice trade**. To expedite trade, this company sought a quicker sea route to Asia. In 1609, it recruited an English sea captain named Henry Hudson to locate a northern passage to the East Indies, a series of key islands in Southeast Asia. Hudson had attempted to find this route before—once in 1607 and again in 1608—but had not succeeded. Nevertheless, he remained convinced such a route existed. In April 1609, Hudson, along with a small crew, assembled on the deck of a ship called the *Halve Maen* (Half Moon) and set off to find it.

Once again, Hudson failed to find a northern route to Asia. He did, however, alight upon an area we now call New

A replica of Henry Hudson's ship, the *Halve Maen* (Half Moon), which was reconstructed in 1989.

York Bay, into which flowed a significant river. Believing this river might lead to a continental (rather than northern) route to the Far East, Hudson followed it.

Hudson called the river the Mauritius River in honor of Maurice, Prince of Orange, Count of Nassau. The Prince of Orange was a Dutch **stadtholder**, or the chief magistrate of the Netherlands. (The Dutch would rename the river the North River. Eventually, it would be christened the Hudson River, after Hudson himself.) The river was, Hudson wrote in his captain's log, "as fine a river as can be found, wide and deep, with good anchoring ground on both sides." As for the land alongside it, it was "the finest for cultivation that I ever in my life set foot upon." That wasn't all. Hudson observed "many skins and peltries [pelts], martins, foxes, and many other commodities." Moreover, the Native people Hudson encountered were, he wrote, "friendly and polite." He wrote this despite the fact that his **vessel** twice came under attack, and one unfortunate member of his crew took an arrow to the throat and died.

Hudson and his crew explored the river for several days. Eventually, near modern-day Troy, New York, the water grew too shallow to continue. Disappointed once again, Hudson turned back and made for Europe—after claiming the land he'd "discovered" for his Dutch employers.

Early Arrivals

Henry Hudson and his crew were not the first people to explore modern-day New York Bay and the Hudson River. They were preceded by Native Americans, who had populated the area since around 10,000 BCE. By the time Hudson arrived, these Native people comprised two main groups: the Iroquois and the Algonquian. Although some Europeans claimed the members of these and other native tribes were "savages," they were, in fact, highly sophisticated, with "a complex and elaborate native economy that included hunting, gathering, manufacturing, and farming."

End of Henry Hudson

Henry Hudson was born in England sometime between 1565 and 1570. Historians believe he started his career at sea as a young man, advancing from cabin boy to sea captain.

Henry Hudson, his son, and others were cast adrift after a mutiny.

After failing to locate a northern passage to Asia in 1609, Hudson became obsessed with finding it. To that end, he set sail once again in 1610. As Hudson and his crew sailed northward, conditions worsened. The ship became trapped in ice. Its sails froze. Crew members contracted frostbite. Food ran dangerously low.

According to one crewman, Abacuk Pricket, "there was not fourteen daies [sic] victual left" and that some of the crew "had not eaten any thing these three dayes [sic]." Still, Hudson pushed on.

Eventually, the crew could take no more. "Resolute … either to mend or end," recalled Pricket, they **mutinied**. They bundled Hudson, seven crewmen who were either sick or had remained loyal to Hudson, and Hudson's young son into a lifeboat and cast it adrift in the freezing waters of what is now Hudson Bay. Hudson and his companions were never seen again.

Native American villages on Manhattan Island consisted of a series of longhouses at the time of the arrival of Dutch colonists.

Indeed, Hudson and his crew weren't even the first *Europeans* to reach New York. In April 1524, Italian explorer Giovanni da Verrazzano entered New York Bay, landing on the tip of modern-day Manhattan Island. (New York City's Verrazano-Narrows Bridge, which connects the boroughs of Brooklyn and Staten Island, is named after this explorer, with a slight change to the spelling of his name.) Eleven years later, a Frenchman named Jacques Cartier passed by en route to the mouth of the St. Lawrence River farther north. But it was the Dutch, inspired by Hudson's "discovery," who claimed and colonized the land in and around what is now New York.

A Shift in Focus

Hudson was disappointed by his failure to locate a northern route to Asia. His employers saw things differently. They were intrigued by Hudson's account of what is now called the New York Harbor and the Hudson River. In particular, the "skins and peltries" mentioned in Hudson's log—in other words, furs and pelts—piqued their interest. There was an enormous

From New Amsterdam to New York:
Dutch Settlement of America

market for these items in Europe. Beaver pelts were particularly prized; hatmakers used them to fashion waterproof hats. Sensing an opportunity, Dutch merchants launched more expeditions into the area. Between 1611 and 1614, Dutch explorers employed by these merchants surveyed and mapped the area, dubbed Nieuw Nederland (New Netherland) after the Dutch homeland, the Netherlands. (The Netherlands is also sometimes called Holland, which technically refers to two of the provinces that comprise the Netherlands.) The new territory stretched from modern-day Massachusetts to Maryland. Later, its boundaries would be adjusted to accommodate English holdings in New England. In addition, these merchants sent representatives to the area to trade with the Native people, mainly for furs. Soon, these merchants aligned to form a new company called the Nieuw Nederland Compagnie (New Netherland Company). In 1614, the Dutch government granted the company a three-year trade **monopoly** in New Netherland. This proved quite profitable.

The First *Factorij*

In 1614, traders built the first Dutch *factorij* (outpost) in the New World. They called it Fort Nassau after the Count of Nassau. The outpost was constructed on a small island in the Hudson River, roughly 7 miles (11.3 kilometers) south of the **confluence** of the Mohawk and Hudson Rivers. Built on the ancestral lands of the native Mohawk and Mohican tribes (also known as the Mahicans), the site gave traders easy access to the fur trade.

The fortification was small—36 feet (11 meters) long by 26 feet (7.9 m) wide, enclosed by a wall and a moat. It housed between ten and twelve men, who defended it with two large cannons and eleven swivel guns. The purpose of the outpost was twofold. First, it was to serve as a warehouse for Dutch fur traders. And second, it was to provide a military defense for those traders.

In 1618, the settlers abandoned Fort Nassau after it was repeatedly flooded. In 1624, they built a replacement, called Fort Orange, 2 miles (3.2 km) to the north. This fortification—despite being described by one visitor as "a miserable little fort"—would endure. Indeed, the site would become modern-day Albany, now capital of the state of New York.

The West India Company

In 1618, the Dutch government declined to renew the monopoly granted to the New Netherland Company. Instead, in 1621, it granted exclusive trade rights in New Netherland to a different company: the Vereenigde West-Indische Compagnie (Dutch West India Company). Moreover, it empowered this company to function as a distinct and separate government abroad. In other words, the Dutch West India Company, not the Dutch government, would appoint governors and other officers, administer justice, make treaties with Native groups, and enact laws in New Netherland.

The Dutch West India Company wanted to populate New Netherland to expand its trade business. This was no easy task. Times were good in seventeenth-century Holland. Few people wanted to leave.

For one thing, Holland was more free, tolerant, and diverse than any other European country. Indeed, as noted by British philosopher Bertrand Russell, "It is impossible to exaggerate the importance of Holland in the seventeenth century, as the one country where there was freedom of speculation." For another, it was prosperous. As historian Russell Shorto notes, it was, "with its paved streets, its scrubbed floors, its wheels of cheese and tankards of excellent beer, its fluffy pillows and blue-and-white tiled hearths and cozy peat fires," comfortable.

Still, some people in Holland—poor people, foreigners, refugees, and the like—were intrigued by the idea of starting fresh somewhere new, particularly after the Dutch West India Company promised them land in exchange for six years of

As seen in *View Of a Marketplace*, Holland was more free, tolerant, diverse, and prosperous than any other European country during the seventeenth century.

service. In 1624, the first of these migrants—a few dozen in all—braved the three-month ocean journey to the New World, landing on the shores of New York Bay.

To maintain control of the land, the Dutch West India Company dispersed these settlers over a wide area. Some stayed on Nut Island (now Governors Island), in New York Bay. Most, however, were taken to various Dutch outposts throughout the region. Some traveled to Fort Orange. Others ventured to Verhulsten Island (now Burlington Island), on what is now the Delaware River. Still others traveled on to Kievitshoek (now Old Saybrook, Connecticut) at the mouth of the Connecticut River. The next year, forty-five more settlers arrived, conveyed by four ships called the *Paert* (Horse), *Koe* (Cow), *Schaep* (Sheep), and *Makreel* (Mackerel)—aptly named, given their additional nonhuman cargo. Like their predecessors, these settlers also dispersed.

Although New Netherland was founded by the Dutch, half the people who ultimately settled there came from elsewhere. Some were Belgian Walloons (a distinct ethnic group in

Belgium). Others were French Huguenots (Protestants). Norwegians, Germans, Italians, Brits, and Bohemians settled in New Netherland. Men and women from Africa also lived there. Most were slaves who had been torn from their homelands by slave traders to work as farmers, builders, and fur traders, although some would eventually gain a sort of "half-free" status. Together, all these settlers braved life in a strange new world.

Under New Management

New Netherland was little more than a Dutch trading outpost. Still, it required governance.

The first leader of New Netherland was a Dutchman named Cornelius Jacobsen May. May was among the first explorers to chart the area beginning in 1614. Later, in 1624, he would captain the ship that brought the first colonists to the area. May knew New Netherland inside and out. When the Dutch West India Company named the province's first director in 1624, May was the natural choice.

May's tenure was brief, however. In 1625, he was replaced by a Dutchman named Willem Verhulst. Alas, Verhulst was widely despised. According to Shorto, Verhulst "meted out harsh and inconsistent punishment, infuriating the colonists." Moreover, "He and his wife may also have misappropriated funds or—an even worse offense—cheated Indians." This was unacceptable. The Dutch West India Company had provided Verhulst with explicit instructions for dealing with the Native people of New Netherland. It commanded him to:

> See that no one do the Indians any harm or violence, deceive, mock, or contemn [sic] them in any way, but that in addition to good treatment they be shown honesty, faithfulness, and sincerity in all contracts, dealings, and intercourse, without being deceived by shortage of measure, weight, or

Director-general of New Netherland Peter Minuit helped the Netherlands shore up its control of its North American colony.

number, and that throughout friendly relations with them be maintained.

Just one year into Verhulst's tenure, a newly formed company-appointed council of settlers voted to banish him from New Netherland. The council then selected a new leader, or director-general: Peter Minuit. Minuit, a scout for the Dutch West India Company, had arrived in New Netherland in 1625, and he had traveled throughout the region. He was, in the words of Shorto, "an individualistic, take-charge sort," and had "spent time in the colony, enough to impress the settlers with his abilities." Minuit would take important steps to solidify Holland's hold on New Netherland.

The Dutch Presence Grows

I nitially, Dutch officials pushed settlers to spread throughout New Netherland, believing it would help to secure the region. Minuit quickly understood that there were too few settlers, spread out across too large of an area, to make this work. Not only was the approach ineffective, it was dangerous. Colonists at Fort Orange had discovered this the previous year. A group of settlers agreed to ally with their Mohican neighbors against a rival tribe, the Mohawks. "In one swift, bloody assault," writes historian Russell Shorto, "a band of ambushing Mohawks put an end to the Dutch-Mahican alliance." Four Dutch settlers and twenty-four Mohicans died in the attack.

Minuit's first decision as director-general was to reverse this practice of dispersal. He relocated many of the colonists who had settled in the far reaches of the region to the southern tip of an island in what is now called New York Bay. The local Lenape tribe called this island Mannahatta, or "hilly island." Mannahatta—modern-day Manhattan Island—was

t' Fort nieúw Amſterdam op de Manhatans

This engraving, called *The Hartgers View*, shows the Dutch settlement that became New Amsterdam on the southern tip of Mannahatta, circa 1626.

an ideal spot, providing easy access to the Atlantic Ocean and an effective way to protect the entrance to the Hudson River, and the fur trade it supported, from outsiders.

It wasn't just the island's location that recommended it. In the words of one early settler in a letter home, the island itself boasted:

> … beautiful rivers, bubbling fountains flowing down into the valleys, basins of running waters in the flatlands, agreeable fruits in the woods, such as strawberries, pigeon berries, walnuts, and also … wild grapes. The woods abound with acorns for feeding hogs, and with venison. There is considerable fish in the rivers; good **tillage** land; here is especially free coming and going, without fear of the naked natives of the country. Had we cows, hogs, and other cattle fit for food (which we daily expect in the first ships) we would not wish to return to Holland, for whatever we desire in the paradise of Holland, it is here to be found.

The Purchase of Manhattan

Dutch settlers were under strict orders to treat the Native people fairly. With that in mind, in 1626, Minuit purchased Mannahatta from the local Lenape tribe, paying sixty guilders' (the equivalent today of about one thousand dollars) worth of goods in exchange for the land. According to lore, these goods consisted of trinkets and beads. More likely, however, they were blankets, knives, kettles, and other useful items.

This may seem like a lousy deal for the Lenape, especially given real-estate prices on modern-day Manhattan. But as noted by Shorto, "the Indians had a different idea of land ownership." He explains, "With no concept of permanent property transfer, Indians of the Northeast saw a real estate deal as a combination of a rental agreement and a treaty or alliance between groups." That meant that "given their idea of land ownership, the Indians who 'sold' Manhattan fully intended to continue to use the land, and they did." It also meant the Dutch were now part of a defensive alliance with the Lenape and were obliged to provide protection against other tribes if needed.

During his tenure as director-general, Minuit would purchase other tracts of land from local tribes on similar terms. These included Staten Island (named for the Staten-Generaal, or States General, which was Holland's governing body), land along the Hudson River to the north, and territory along the Delaware River to the south.

Life in New Amsterdam

In time, the settlement—christened Nieuw Amsterdam (New Amsterdam)—would become the region's capital and main port. Indeed, within a year of its founding, it boasted thirty wooden houses, one stone building, and two windmills— one to grind grain and one to saw lumber. The settlers also constructed a fort, called Fort Amsterdam, which contained

Director-general Peter Minuit purchased Mannahatta from the local Lenape tribe for the price of sixty guilders' worth of goods.

a **barracks**, a church, a warehouse, and living quarters for the director-general.

Over the next thirty years, New Amsterdam would grow from a settlement sheltering a few dozen Dutch colonists and trappers to a multicultural municipality. According to Jesuit priest Father Isaac Jogues, who visited New Amsterdam in 1643, "on the island of Manhattan there may well be four or five hundred people of different sects and nations: the Director-General told me that there were persons of eighteen different languages."

New Netherland was a remarkably free society— especially compared to the English colonies to the north, whose members practiced a strict form of Protestantism (and banished anyone who did otherwise). Technically, the official religion of New Netherland was the Dutch Reformed Church, a **Calvinist** religion. But, as noted by Father Jogues, "besides the Calvinists, there are Catholics, English Puritans, Lutherans, Anabaptists (Mennonites) and more in the colony." This religious tolerance was in keeping with Dutch views.

For the most part, this diverse population coexisted peacefully. According to Father Jogues, "When anyone comes to settle in the country, they lend him horses, cows, etc.; they give him provisions, which he all returns as soon as he is at ease." The population also prospered—particularly after 1640. That year, the Dutch West India Company declared New Netherland a free trading zone. In other words, *anyone* was free to engage in trade, not just company men. New Amsterdam soon became a trading giant, the hub of North American shipping. Suddenly, goods of all kinds—food, timber, tobacco, and, shamefully, slaves—passed through the area. This spawned, in Shorto's words, a sort of "freeform upward mobility that American culture would inherit from its forgotten colony."

The Patroon System

The population of New Netherland grew, but not quickly enough for the Dutch West India Company. To attract more settlers, the company issued the Charter of Freedoms and Exemptions in 1629. This **charter** offered large tracts of land to anyone who could recruit fifty colonists to work the property. These landowners, called **patroons**, were free to manage the land and its inhabitants as they saw fit. For example, they could create their own civil and criminal courts and appoint their own local officials. Their only real obligation to the company (apart from recruiting the settlers) was to ship any goods produced on the land to New Amsterdam rather than trading them elsewhere, and to refrain from engaging in the fur trade in any areas already claimed by the company.

In all, the Dutch West India Company issued just five of these charters. The largest and most successful patroonship, as the resulting settlements were called, was Rensselaerswyck,

From New Amsterdam to New York:
Dutch Settlement of America

near Fort Orange. Owned by a Dutch merchant named Kiliaen van Rensselaer, the property eventually grew to cover several hundred thousand acres. Father Jogues described the settlement: "This colony is composed of about one hundred persons, who reside in some twenty-five or thirty houses built along the river … All their houses are merely of boards and thatched with no mason work except the chimneys." The chief occupation of these residents was farming, despite there being "little land fit for tillage, being hemmed in by hills, which have poor soil." However, "They found already some pieces of ground, which the savages had formerly cleared, in which they sow wheat and oats for beer and their horses, of which they have a great number."

These charters seemed like a good idea. Eventually, however, the company would regret their issue. Despite the company's best efforts, it simply could not maintain control over the flow of trade from these properties. Residents frequently engaged in illegal commerce, keeping for themselves profits that should have gone to the company.

Minuit's Fall from Grace

In 1631, the Dutch West India Company suspended Peter Minuit from his post and recalled him to Europe. The reason for this action is unclear—particularly considering Minuit's accomplishments as director-general. In just five years, Minuit had solidified Dutch holdings in New Netherland; fostered good relationships with local tribes; overseen the shipment of tens of thousands of pelts and other valuable goods to Europe; and established the colony's capital.

In Minuit's place, the Dutch West India Company installed a young clerk named Wouter van Twiller. Van Twiller had, says Shorto, "no particular set of skills to recommend him, only a dull devotion to the company and a family relation to an important man connected with the colony." Worse, he was a "drunk" and a "nonleader."

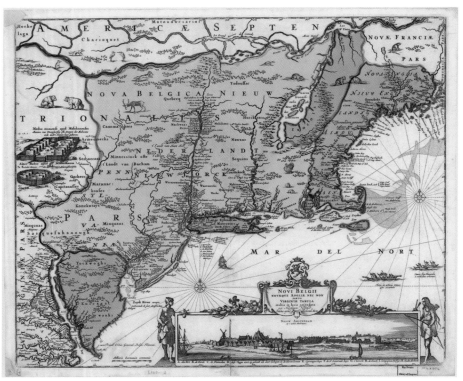

This map of New Netherland, drawn in 1656 and reprinted in 1685, shows the division of the land among the nations.

If van Twiller was bad, his successor, Willem Kieft—who assumed leadership of the colony in 1638—was even worse. Incompetent and impulsive, Kieft acted more like a dictator than a director. This, the colonists would soon discover, would prove deadly.

Encroaching Enemies

It would be against Kieft that Minuit would enjoy a sweet revenge. In 1638, with the support of the Swedish government, Minuit launched a new colony called Nya Sverige (New Sweden) on the Delaware River—squarely within Dutch territory. Led by Minuit, the Swedish colonists constructed a fort, called Fort Christina after Queen Christina of Sweden. Minuit perished at sea soon after.

Kiliaen van Rensselaer

K iliaen van Rensselaer was born in 1586. His father was a soldier, and his mother was a descendant of a well-known family of printers. After serving as an **apprentice** for his uncle, a successful jeweler in Amsterdam, Van Rensselaer became a wealthy diamond and pearl merchant. He was also one of the founders of the Dutch West India Company.

Although Van Rensselaer was the patroon of Rensselaerswyck, he did not live there. Rather, he remained in Holland. Still, he expected residents of Rensselaerswyck to swear their allegiance to him. He was, says Shorto, "universally feared and respected as a kind of latter-day medieval prince." Indeed, letters to Van Rensselaer often contained the fawning salutation "Most honorable, wise, powerful, and right discreet Lord."

Van Rensselaer, who married twice, fathered at least eleven children. He died sometime after 1642, leaving his estate in New Netherland to his sons. Under their stewardship, and that of later managers, Rensselaerswyck would grow to cover nearly a million acres and employ one hundred thousand tenant farmers.

However, the Swedish colony lived on, eventually extending 100 miles (160 km) up the Delaware River valley. For years, it would remain a thorn in the side of Kieft and his successor.

Meanwhile, the Massachusetts Bay Colony, founded by English settlers in 1628, had taken root in the north. To van Twiller's and, later, Kieft's great alarm, some members of that population had moved southward. In 1636, roughly one hundred Puritans, led by a preacher named Thomas Hooker, settled in modern-day Hartford, Connecticut—territory that had previously been claimed and colonized by the Dutch. This was despite gestures of friendship to the then-struggling English made during Minuit's reign, including the delivery of "a rundlet of sugar, and two Holland cheeses."

Kieft's War

In Kieft's mind, New Netherland faced yet another enemy: the Native population. He didn't think they posed a threat to the colony per se. Rather, he believed they endangered the solvency of the Dutch West India Company. Simply put, the Dutch West India Company could no longer afford to protect the tribes from whom it had purchased land and with whom it had established defensive alliances. That, combined with the siphoning of profits from the various patroons, had imperiled the company's finances.

Kieft's solution to this problem was to tax the Native people for defensive services rendered, as outlined in this directive:

> Whereas the Company is put to great expense both in building fortifications and in supporting soldiers and sailors, we have therefore resolved to demand from the Indians who dwell around here and whom heretofore we have protected against their enemies, some contributions in the form of skins, maize and seawan, and if there be any nation which is not in a friendly way disposed to make such a contribution it shall be urged to do so in the most suitable manner.

This proved ineffective. Indeed, several local chiefs simply laughed at the directive. Humiliated, Kieft lashed out, falsely accusing members of the nearby Raritan tribe of stealing hogs from a farm on Staten Island. In fact, the thieves were

From New Amsterdam to New York:
Dutch Settlement of America

Director-general William Kieft and colleagues plot a catastrophic war against local tribes.

colonists. To retaliate for this "theft," Kieft sent a posse to the tribe's village. Several tribe members were killed.

Now the cycle of violence escalated. First, a group of Raritan burned down the farm from which the hogs were stolen. Then, a member of a rival tribe decapitated the Raritan chief. But it was an unrelated incident that brought the conflict to a tipping point. In August 1641, a settler named Claes Swits was brutally murdered by a member of the Wickquasgeck tribe. It was a random killing. Years before, several Europeans had robbed and murdered a small group of the Wickquasgeck, leaving just one young survivor. Fifteen years later, that young survivor murdered Swits—who had not been involved in the earlier incident—in revenge. This gave Kieft all the ammunition he needed.

MASSACRE OF INDIANS AT HOBOKEN.

Dutch soldiers massacred local Native Americans near current day Hoboken, New Jersey, in Kieft's War.

In February 1643, against the wishes of the colonists and of the council of men they had elected to represent them in this matter, Kieft launched a surprise attack on a nearby Native camp. Of the massacre, often called Kieft's War, one colonist wrote:

> Infants were torn from their mother's breasts, and hacked to pieces in the presence of their parents, and the pieces thrown into the fire and in the water, and other sucklings, being bound to small boards, were cut, stuck, and pierced, and miserably massacred in a manner to move a heart of stone. Some were thrown into the river,

and when the fathers and mothers endeavored to save them, the soldiers would not let them come on land but made both parents and children drown.

The Dutch had coexisted in relative peace with tribes throughout New Netherland, including the Algonquian, Mohican, Mohawk, Lenape, Wickquasgeck, Hackensack, Raritan, Canarsee, Tappan, Munsee and Minqua. This was due in part to the colonists' relatively enlightened view of these Native people. Alas, thanks to Kieft, this relative peace was over. Indeed, according to Shorto, "Kieft's action had brought about something that heretofore had been unachievable: the unification of area tribes into a confederation, one aimed at slaughtering Europeans." Shorto continues, "Attacks came without warning, in the deep of night." Now, due to Kieft's foolishness, the very existence of the Dutch colony was at risk.

Colonists Versus the Company

Kieft's War—conducted against the colonists' wishes—
proved unwise. For two years, colonists found
themselves under attack by nearby tribes. Many
colonists were killed. Others were driven from their homes
and their livelihoods. With each assault, their anger mounted.

To calm the colonists, Kieft proposed the formation of a
new council of representatives. Somewhat soothed, the colonists
assented. They even agreed to let Kieft choose the members of
the council. As any poor leader would do, Kieft assembled a
body of men he believed would back him. He miscalculated. The
board did not offer its unconditional support—something Kieft
discovered after proposing a tax on beavers and beer. The council
met this proposal with howls of protest.

The council's argument was twofold. First, many of the
people Kieft intended to tax were the very ones who had lost

Cornelis Melyn trades with members of local tribes on Staten Island in part of a
mural from the Staten Island Borough Hall.

their homes and livelihoods. Second, they believed Kieft could not impose such a tax without authorization from the Dutch West India Company headquarters in Holland. A popular uprising ensued. The colonists were particularly outraged by the beer tax. As historian Russell Shorto observes, "The people refused to pay it, and the tavern keepers refused to charge it."

Two members of the council, Jochem Kuyter and Cornelis Melyn, decided to write to the directors of the Dutch West India Company in Holland to complain. For help, they tapped one Adriaen van der Donck, who was a lawyer by trade. Van der Donck composed a powerful letter. First, the letter described the events leading up to Kieft's War, noting that Kieft "commenced the war against those of Wesquecqueck, on his own mere mention." Next, it questioned the legality of Kieft's attempts at taxation, railing against the notion "that one man … should dispose here of our lives and properties at his will and pleasure, in a manner so arbitrary that a King dare not legally do the like." Finally, it called for the formation of a representative government, in which colonists "elect from among themselves a Bailiff or Schout [scout] and Schepens [judges], who will be empowered to send their deputies and give their votes on public affairs with the Director and Council; so that the entire country may not be hereafter, at the whim of one man, again reduced to similar danger." A colleague then smuggled this letter to Holland.

In some respects, this letter was effective. It persuaded the directors of the Dutch West India Company to kill the proposed taxes and to fire Kieft. But in others, it only made things worse. After reading the letter, the directors opted against granting the colonists popular representation. Instead, they cracked down. Soon, they installed a new leader—one who would prove formidable indeed.

From New Amsterdam to New York:
Dutch Settlement of America

Forces Collide

Adriaen van der Donck studied law at Leiden University. There, he no doubt read the work of Hugo Grotius and Cunaeus. Their writings would shape the views of future thinkers about the rights of people (innate, based on natural law) and the optimal form of government (representative democracy). The ideals encapsulated in these writings would go on to influence many scholars and thinkers, including van der Donck and the Founding Fathers of the United States.

These ideals stood in sharp contrast with reality, at least in New Netherland. The Dutch West India Company maintained absolute rule over the colony. Colonists weren't constituents of the Dutch Republic. They were subjects of the Dutch West India Company. The director-general of the colony, appointed by the company, had absolute authority over them. His job was to protect the company's interests, not the rights of colonists. This, notes Shorto, "was an accepted business model in the seventeenth century." He continues, "In most situations in which the East and West India Companies found themselves, it worked."

There were opposing forces working in the colony. There was a company trying to build a business empire, and there were political philosophers whose views were reflected by people such as van der Donck. These two forces collided in New Netherland.

For more than two decades, the colonists fought for a role in their own governance as Dutch citizens. This role would change the political system and put property in which the Dutch West India Company shareholders had invested heavily under government control. And for more than two decades, the Dutch West India Company fought back. Precedent was on their side. Running profitable trading posts in other countries was an accepted practice in the Dutch system.

Sadly, in the end, neither side would prevail.

Director-general Peter Stuyvesant attempted social reforms when he arrived in New Netherland.

From New Amsterdam to New York:
Dutch Settlement of America

The Arrival of Peter Stuyvesant

In May 1647, the colony's new leader, Peter Stuyvesant, arrived in New Amsterdam. Stuyvesant was an imposing figure, although hobbled by a wooden peg where his right leg used to be. While commanding a military assault on behalf of the Dutch West India Company on a Portuguese-held island in the Caribbean three years prior, Stuyvesant had taken a "rough ball," or cannonball, to the leg, shattering it beyond repair. Doctors had no choice but to amputate—a procedure that, in those days, was performed without anesthesia.

The son of a grim Calvinist minister, Stuyvesant was a born leader. He joined the Dutch West India Company as a clerk sometime around 1635. By 1642, he had risen to the post of director-general of the colony of Curaçao—a position he held until his injury two years later. Now, having fully recovered, Stuyvesant was ready for his next challenge, as director-general of New Netherland.

Stuyvesant was, in the words of Shorto, "smart, deep, honest, and narrow." He was also horrified by the level of disorder in New Netherland. The population's less respectable members, including pirates, smugglers, and sharks, sometimes fueled mayhem. Compounding this was the ready availability of alcohol. In New Amsterdam, one in every four buildings housed a tavern or a brewery. It was, says Shorto, the type of place where, "with nightfall, the soft slap of waves along the shore was drowned out by drinking songs and angry curses." Perhaps not surprisingly, "the records are rife with murderous assaults."

The Sunday after Stuyvesant's arrival in New Amsterdam, a drunken knife fight erupted. This prompted his first edict, forbidding tavern owners from selling alcohol on Sundays until after church because of "the insolence of some of our inhabitants, when drunk," which led to "their quarreling, hitting and fighting each other even on the Lord's day of rest." Alcohol would pose a persistent problem for Stuyvesant, who believed it caused "not only the neglect of honest handicraft and business, but also the debauching of the common man and the Company's servants and what is still worse, of the young people from childhood up, who seeing the improper proceedings of their parents and imitating them leave the path of virtue and become disorderly." Clearly, New Netherland had been terribly mismanaged. Stuyvesant was determined to change that.

Kieft, Kuyter, and Melyn

Stuyvesant would indeed bring order to New Amsterdam—and to the rest of New Netherland, which had, over time, welcomed more settlers. But he had one other top priority: punishing Jochem Kuyter and Cornelis Melyn. Their signatures appeared at the bottom of the letter that called for Kieft's ousting—an act that Stuyvesant viewed as nothing less than treason. To seek justice, Stuyvesant vowed to formally review the case.

In June 1647, Stuyvesant assembled the aggrieved parties—Kieft on one side, and Kuyter and Melyn on the other. He expected a swift and decisive meeting, one in which everyone would sit and listen to him say how things would be run, and then he would pass judgment. Instead, Kuyter, Melyn, and other colonists (including van der Donck) presented him with "long lists of questions, together with demands that they be posed to the parties indicated and a call for the reorganization of the colony," according to Shorto.

A series of events then occurred to ratchet things up. First, Stuyvesant showed Kieft the offending letter sent by Kuyter and Melyn to Holland, which Kieft had never seen. Kieft, enraged, wrote a formal complaint, accusing Kuyter and Melyn of **libel**. He demanded that the two men be sent to Holland to be tried "as pests and seditious persons." In response, Kuyter and Melyn, with van der Donck's help, wrote a new letter rebutting Kieft's charges and demanding that Kuyter and Melyn return to Holland not to be tried, but to testify on their own behalf "as good patriots and proprietors of New Netherland." At stake was not a single incident but a ruling on the rights of Dutch citizens who were in an outpost far from home. The protagonists knew this would be a test case. As the letter demanded, "Let us then once see what the law of nations thinks of it."

Ultimately, Stuyvesant sent all three men—Kieft, Kuyter, and Melyn—to Holland. Incredibly, their ship, the *Princess Amelia*, wrecked off the coast of Wales. Eighty-six lives were lost. Presumably among the dead were Kieft, Kuyter, and Melyn. With the three men seemingly out of the picture, Stuyvesant was at last free to lead as he saw fit.

Threats

Liberated from the distraction posed by Kieft, Kuyter, and Melyn, Stuyvesant assessed the security of the colony. Of late, the threat posed by local Native people—which had escalated sharply during Kieft's War—had diminished. This was in large part due to a peace treaty signed by Kieft himself in 1645. The treaty—ordered by the Dutch West India Company, brokered by Adriaen van der Donck, and cosigned by representatives of the Hackensack, Tappan, Rechgawawanck, Nyack, and Wickquasgeck tribes—called for "a firm and inviolable peace" and for future disputes to be settled through communication rather than carnage.

Another threat nagged at Stuyvesant: New Sweden, the colony founded by Peter Minuit. New Sweden was too small to assert itself against New Netherland. However, if some other, more powerful group were to gain control over the area—say, the English—it would be another story. To prevent this, Stuyvesant ordered the purchase of neighboring lands from the local tribes and the repair and restock of all Dutch forts in the area.

The English, Stuyvesant knew, were the real threat. This was particularly true of the four New England colonies to the north: Connecticut, New Haven, New Plymouth, and

After leaving New Netherland, Peter Minuit helped establish New Sweden and Fort Christina. Part of the reconstructed fort is shown above.

Massachusetts. To neutralize this threat, Stuyvesant proposed a treaty whose main purpose would be to outline permanent land boundaries. In this, Stuyvesant prevailed—although not right away. It took three years.

The Board of Nine

In addition to these outside threats, Stuyvesant had to contend with matters closer to home. He needed to oversee the

From New Amsterdam to New York: Dutch Settlement of America

renovation of Fort Amsterdam, which had fallen into disrepair, and the construction of, in his words, "a school, church, sheet piling, pier and similar highly necessary public works and common buildings." For that, he would, of course, need funds—and for funds, he would need the support of the colonists.

To gain this support, Stuyvesant allowed the formation of a new advisory group of representatives. Colonists elected eighteen candidates for the group, from which Stuyvesant selected nine members—hence its name, the Board of Nine. (This group was separate from Stuyvesant's council, which represented the company.)

Events would soon lead Stuyvesant—whose leadership style was more authoritative than collaborative—to regret the assembly of this board.

CHAPTER FOUR

The End of New Netherland

S oon after their appointment, members of the Board of Nine—led by van der Donck—quickly drafted a petition asking to send a representative to Holland. The purpose of this visit would be to appeal to the Dutch government to wrest control of New Netherland from the Dutch West India Company. Infuriated, Stuyvesant ignored the petition.

Soon, something happened that Stuyvesant couldn't ignore. Jochem Kuyter and Cornelis Melyn—presumed drowned following the wreck of the *Princess Amelia*—returned to New Netherland, very much alive. They brought with them a **mandamus** from the Dutch government. This document condemned "the war that Director Kieft illegally and contrary to all public Law, had commenced against the Indians." (Of course, this was moot, Kieft having *actually* drowned at sea.) It also approved the election of popular representatives to avoid such catastrophes in the future. Finally, it **exonerated** Kuyter and Melyn and recalled Stuyvesant (or a representative) to Holland to explain himself.

Stuyvesant was irate. His fury mounted when he discovered that the Board of Nine was canvassing residents of New Amsterdam to gauge whether they did indeed support government reform. (They did.) Stuyvesant ordered a search of the home of one board member. This uncovered a **dossier** of grievances laid out by various colonists and a draft of a **brief** making the case for reform—both bearing the mark of Adriaen van der Donck. Stuyvesant arrested van der Donck and charged him with high treason—a crime punishable by death.

No doubt, Stuyvesant would have preferred simply to execute van der Donck and be done with the matter. But he lacked the support of the Board of Nine, and even of members of his own council. Therefore, he released van der Donck and ordered him to "prove and establish or to revoke what he has injuriously written."

Van der Donck chose to prove his case. He assembled all the information that the Board of Nine had gathered into an eighty-three-page complaint. He then arranged, along with two other board members, to travel to Holland, where he would present it to the States General. Not to be outdone, Stuyvesant sent a representative of his own to plead his case. "Who the delinquent is," Stuyvesant wrote to van der Donck in a strained message, "God and the law have to decide."

A Stunning Victory

Van der Donck and his colleagues arrived in Holland in October 1649 and quickly won an audience with the States General. There, he presented the document he had so painstakingly composed, titled "**Remonstrance** of New Netherland, and the Occurrences There, Addressed to the High and Mighty Lords States General of the United Netherlands, by the People of New Netherland." The document's primary aim was the establishment of "suitable municipal government"—a requirement if the colony were to continue to grow.

The response of the States General wasn't immediate. But when it finally came—in April 1650—it represented a stunning victory for van der Donck and the Board of Nine. It stated that members of the States General "cannot, and ought not any longer approve of the perverse administration of the privileges and benefits granted by charter to the stockholders of the West India Company [while] neglecting or opposing the good plans and offers submitted for the security of the boundaries and the increase of the population of that country." Moreover, the States General ordered that a municipal government be installed in New Amsterdam (and that the Board of Nine maintain jurisdiction until said government could be organized). Finally, it repeated its call for the return of Peter Stuyvesant to Holland—something van der Donck hadn't even requested.

A Crushing Defeat

Van der Donck's colleagues returned to New Netherland. Van der Donck, however, remained in Holland to finalize the details surrounding the States General's decision. He would remain far longer than expected—some four years in all. Worse, due to events completely outside his control, he would return to New Netherland in utter defeat.

The cause of this turn in fortunes was the advent of the First Anglo-Dutch War (1652–1654). In this brief conflict, England—led by Oliver Cromwell, whose "roundheads" had won the English Civil War (1642–1651) and removed the British monarchy (or, more precisely, the British monarch's head)—struck at the Dutch in an attempt to break their monopoly on trade in Europe, Asia, and North America. For all practical purposes, this conflict, most of which was carried out at sea, ended in a draw.

From New Amsterdam to New York:
Dutch Settlement of America

Interior of the Great Hall on the Binnenhof in The Hague, during the Assembly of the States-General in 1651 depicts the scene faced by Adriaen van der Donck.

There was one clear winner in the war, however: the Dutch West India Company. When van der Donck and his colleagues pleaded their case in front of the States General, the Dutch West India Company was widely regarded as a flop. Its share price, which had peaked at 206 guilders, had plunged to 14 guilders. But things were different now. The Dutch were at war. Suddenly, notes Shorto, "the company, which after all had originally been conceived as a quasi-military entity, came roaring back to life." Under pressure from the Dutch West India Company, and suddenly fearful of enacting more liberal reforms, "the States General completely reversed its rulings on the Manhattan-based colony." For his part, van der Donck "was no longer a patriot but a radical, someone to keep watch on." He was therefore detained in Holland. When van der Donck was at last permitted to return to New Netherland in 1653, it was under several conditions—chief among these that he would, in his own words, "accept no office whatever it may be" and "[submit] to the orders and commands of the Company or those enacted by its director."

New Sweden Falls

With van der Donck, his chief rival, neutralized, Stuyvesant turned his attention to New Sweden. He planned to rid himself of this upstart adversary once and for all. In the late summer of 1655, backed by six hundred men, Stuyvesant sailed to New Sweden. The Swedes, considerably outmanned, quickly surrendered.

This event would have one unintended and unfortunate consequence. Within days of Stuyvesant's victory over New Sweden, six hundred Native Americans landed on the southern tip of New Amsterdam. They ran through the streets, shooting arrows and destroying things with their axes. Then they raided areas to the north on the mainland and on Staten Island. They burned homes, killed several dozen

The First Anglo-Dutch War was fought primarily at sea. The war boosted the fortunes of the Dutch West India Company.

settlers, and took hostages. At first, settlers believed this raid had occurred in retaliation for the murder of a Native woman who had stolen peaches from a Dutch settler. That's why the incident was called the Peach War. In fact, it appears to have been a direct result of Stuyvesant's dismantling of the Swedish colony. The Native Americans, Shorto wrote, "had devoted seventeen years to cultivating a trading relationship with the Swedes, only to see Stuyvesant and his soldiers destroy it. So the Indians retaliated." Sadly, it's believed that Adriaen van der Donck was among the settlers killed during the Peach War.

The English Take Over

The next ten years passed in relative peace. Trade flourished, more settlers came, and New Amsterdam expanded. That peace would soon pass, however.

The series of events that led to this change began in 1658. That year, Oliver Cromwell died. This sparked a political crisis, which ended with the restoration of the British monarchy in 1660.

The new king, Charles II, was a man of varied interests. Governing, however, was not high among them. His younger brother, James, the Duke of York, was different. James envisioned a more powerful England, one that defeated the Dutch once and for all. James convinced Charles to support a new campaign against the Netherlands.

A key part of this campaign was the acquisition of New Netherland. To that end, King Charles II simply deeded the land to the New England Confederation. Formed in 1654, the Confederation included the Massachusetts, Plymouth, Connecticut, and New Haven colonies. Charles soon changed his mind, however, and gifted the land to his brother James.

Of this, the Dutch had no knowledge—but they learned of the plot soon enough. In August 1664, four English gunboats, sent by the Duke of York and led by one Richard

James, Duke of York

James, Duke of York, was born in 1633, the second son of King Charles I. In 1660, he married a commoner, Anne Hyde. Anne bore eight children. Only two survived: Mary and little Anne. In 1669, James and Anne converted to the Roman Catholic Church. Charles II allowed the conversion, but he insisted Mary and little Anne be raised Protestant. In 1671, Anne died. James remarried in 1673. His second wife was Mary of Modena, a fifteen-year-old Italian princess.

James, Duke of York, before he became King James II.

Charles II died in 1685, leaving no legitimate heir. James assumed the throne as King James II. This upset the nobility, who were overwhelmingly Protestant. They persuaded William of Orange—who had married the king's Protestant daughter Mary—to overthrow James. In 1688, William of Orange obliged, in an invasion now called the Glorious Revolution. James fled to Ireland, thereby abdicating the throne to his daughter Mary, who ruled alongside her husband.

James never reclaimed the English throne. Nor did he ever visit his colony in the New World. He died in France in 1701.

The fall of New Amsterdam happened without a shot being fired as the citizens petitioned Peter Stuyvesant to surrender.

From New Amsterdam to New York:
Dutch Settlement of America

Nicolls, cruised into the harbor at New Amsterdam. Nicolls presented his demands to Stuyvesant:

> In his Majesties Name, I do demand the Towne, Scituate upon the Island commonly knowne by the Name of Manhatoes with all the Forts there unto belonging, to be rendered unto his Majesties obedience, and Protection into my hands [or face] the miseryes of a War.

Nicolls's terms were lenient—even generous. And the Dutch were outmanned two to one. Still, Stuyvesant intended to fight to the death. He soon realized, however, that he was the only one. The townspeople circulated a petition demanding that Stuyvesant yield to prevent "misery, sorrow, **conflagration**, the dishonor of women, murder of children in their cradles, and, in a word, the absolute ruin and destruction of about fifteen hundred innocent souls." Stuyvesant had no choice but to surrender.

Without a shot being fired, without a life being lost, New Amsterdam became New York. And except for one brief period (1673–1674), during which the Dutch reclaimed the city (this time renaming it New Orange after the Prince of Orange), so it would remain.

The Legacy of the Dutch

New Netherland fell to the English. Still, the legacy of the Dutch in the New World—particularly in and around New York City—lives on.

This legacy can be found in place names, like Brooklyn (Breuckelen), the Bronx (Bronck), Staten Island (Staten Eylandt), and Yonkers (Jonker). This last is of particular note. *Jonker* was the Dutch word for "squire," an **epithet** for Adriaen van der Donck used by many of his New Amsterdam neighbors. It was in modern-day Yonkers that van der

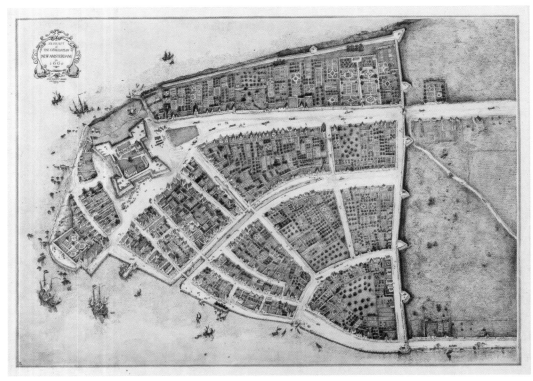

The Castello Plan, the earliest known map of New Amsterdam, was made in 1660. You can see Broadway and Wall Street, which was really a wall.

Donck's farm was built. Other Dutch words have survived, too—words like cookie (*koekje*) and boss (*baas*)—perhaps because inhabitants in the region continued to speak that language for some time.

Another example of this legacy can be seen in the frequent use of blue, white, and orange—the colors of the Dutch flag during the seventeenth century—throughout the region. The New York Knicks sport these colors on the basketball court (a Knickerbocker is a descendant of the region's early Dutch settlers), as do the New York Islanders hockey club and the New York Mets baseball team. These colors also appear in the official flag of New York City. (The city's seal, which appears

From New Amsterdam to New York: Dutch Settlement of America

The official flag of New York City reflects the colors of the Dutch flag, and the seal of the city includes the date of the founding of New Amsterdam.

on this flag, contains another Dutch reference: the year New Amsterdam was founded.)

Perhaps the most significant legacy of New Netherland is its cultural legacy. It was New Netherland that introduced ideals like religious tolerance, cultural diversity, upward mobility, and even civil liberties to the New World. These ideals would live on in the region—eventually spreading across the continent and even defining the new nation of the United States of America. For these contributions, all Americans owe their thanks.

Chronology

Dates in green pertain to events discussed in this volume.

October 31, 1517: Martin Luther posts his "The 95 Theses" on a church door in Germany, starting a religious revolution known as "The Reformation."

1534: England ends its formal association with the Catholic Church and forms the Church of England, with King Henry VIII as its leader.

April 10, 1606: King James I issues the First Virginia Charter to the Virginia Company, authorizing its leaders to establish the Virginia colony and beginning the Colonial period.

May 13, 1607: The first permanent English colony in the New World is established at Jamestown, Virginia.

1609: Henry Hudson discovers what we now call the New York Bay and the Hudson River.

July 30, 1619: The House of Burgesses, the first legislative assembly in the colonies, convenes.

September 6, 1620: The *Mayflower* leaves Plymouth, England, for North America.

November 9, 1620: The Pilgrims see land for the first time on their trip; it is Cape Cod.

November 11, 1620: Adult males on the *Mayflower* sign the Mayflower Compact.

December 21, 1620: The Pilgrims land in Plymouth, Massachusetts.

Fall 1621: The Pilgrims and the Wampanoag celebrate a fall harvest festival together in what is considered the first Thanksgiving celebration in America.

November 9, 1621: The *Fortune* arrives in Plymouth, carrying additional people but no supplies.

May 1624: The Dutch establish the colony of New Netherland.

1626: Peter Minuit takes command of New Netherland, purchases the island of Mannahatta (modern-day Manhattan) on behalf of the Dutch, and begins construction on New Amsterdam.

March 4, 1629: The Massachusetts Bay Company

receives a charter from Charles I to trade in New England.

June 12, 1630: Puritan leaders of the Massachusetts Bay Company land at Salem.

1632: Charles I grants to Lord Baltimore territory north of the Potomac River, which becomes Maryland; the king does not restrict residency to Protestants, so Catholics are allowed.

March 3, 1634: The *Ark* and the *Dove* sail up the Chesapeake Bay, carrying the first settlers of Maryland; on March 25, the group purchases land from the Natives and names its settlement St. Mary's.

June 1636: Roger Williams founds the colony of Rhode Island.

1636: Puritans settle in modern-day Connecticut—territory that had been claimed by the Dutch.

1638: Peter Minuit, former leader of New Netherland, establishes New Sweden squarely within Dutch territory.

1655: Peter Stuyvesant, leader of New Netherland, defeats New Sweden.

1664: King Charles II of England deeds the territory of New Netherland to his brother, the Duke of York (despite having no legal authority to do so).

September 7, 1664: The Dutch surrender New Amsterdam to the English, who rename the colony New York.

September 1664: A statute denying freedom to slaves who converted to Christianity is passed in Maryland; Virginia passes a similar measure in 1667.

1673: The Dutch briefly reclaim New York, only to lose it again the next year.

June 24, 1675: The Native population attacks Swansea, Massachusetts, at the start of an attempt to wipe out the English settlers with a massive military action. This starts King Philip's War.

August 12, 1676: King Philip's War ends.

September 19, 1676: Jamestown is burned during Bacon's Rebellion; the rebellion ends the next month following the death of its leader, Nathaniel Bacon.

March 4, 1681: Charles II grants William Penn a charter for what becomes Pennsylvania.

May 1689: King William's War, the first French and Indian War, begins with the British declaring war on France; the war ends in 1697 with the Treaty of Ryswick.

October 7, 1691: The Province of Massachusetts Bay is chartered, merging the Massachusetts Bay Colony with the Maine and Plymouth territories to form a larger colony.

June 8, 1692: The Plymouth General Council has its last meeting.

May 4, 1702: Queen Anne's War, the second French and Indian War, begins.

February 29, 1704: French and Indian forces kill fifty residents and take more than one hundred captives in a raid on Deerfield, Massachusetts.

September 22, 1711: The Tuscarora Indian War begins in North Carolina; surviving Native Americans move north to New York to join the League of Six Nations.

April 11, 1713: Queen Anne's War ends as France signs the Treaty of Utrecht. France cedes Newfoundland and Nova Scotia to Britain.

April 21, 1732: King George signs a charter creating Georgia and establishes a board of trustees to govern the colony.

April 3, 1735: Britain ratifies an act banning slavery in Georgia.

September 9, 1739: Slaves in South Carolina begin the Stono Rebellion, which ends with between forty-two and forty-seven whites and forty-four blacks killed; it is the largest slave rebellion in the colonies.

April 21, 1741: A jury is impaneled to hear testimony on an alleged plot to burn New York City; this incident was termed the Great Negro Plot of 1741 and the New York Conspiracy of 1741.

January 1, 1751: A resolution passed by the state's House of Commons to allow slavery in Georgia takes effect.

May 28, 1754: Troops representing France and Great Britain and their Native American allies battle at Fort Duquesne in a struggle for control of the Ohio River Valley. This is the first fighting in what becomes the Seven Years' War, otherwise known as the French and Indian War.

May 15, 1756: Britain declares war on France, officially starting the French and Indian War.

September 13, 1759: British forces capture Quebec City in the climactic battle of the French and Indian War; the leaders of both armies, General Louis-Joseph de Montcalm of the French and Commander James Wolfe of the British, die in the fighting.

February 10, 1763: The signing of the Treaty of Paris ends the French and Indian War. This closes the Colonial period.

Glossary

apprentice Someone who works for a fixed period at a low wage to learn a trade from a skilled employer.

barracks A building for housing a specific group of people, usually soldiers.

brief A document that provides a concise summary of a topic.

Calvinist A person who adheres to a form of Protestantism devised by John Calvin and his followers. It teaches, among other things, the total depravity of mankind (sin reaches every part of a person's personality) and the doctrine of predestination.

charter A grant issued by a governing body or other power that defines the rights and privileges of the grantee.

conflagration A great fire that destroys significant swaths of land or property.

confluence The point at which two or more rivers meet.

dossier A collection of documents that pertain to a specific person, topic, or happening.

epithet A word or phrase that describes and may even come to identify a person.

exonerate To clear someone of blame.

libel A false published statement that damages someone's reputation.

From New Amsterdam to New York:
Dutch Settlement of America

mandamus A document that orders someone to perform a public duty.

monopoly The state of having complete control over a particular area of trade.

mutiny To refuse to submit to the commands of a person of authority, usually by soldiers or sailors against their officers.

patroon A proprietor of a large manor and estate, mostly in what is now New York, granted under the Dutch.

remonstrance A document that forcefully and formally spells out reasons for opposition or protest.

spice trade The trade of goods and spices, such as cinnamon, cardamom, ginger, and pepper, among countries in Asia, Africa, and Europe.

stadtholder The title given the chief magistrate of the Netherlands.

tillage The preparation of land needed to cultivate crops or land under cultivation.

vessel A ship or a large boat.

Further Information

Books

Fabend, Firth Haring. *New Netherland in a Nutshell: A Concise History of the Dutch Colony in North America*. Albany, NY: New Netherland Institute, 2012.

Krizner, L. J., and Lisa Sita. *Peter Stuyvesant: New Amsterdam and the Origins of New York*. New York: Rosen Publishing, 2001.

Shorto, Russell. *The Island at the Center of the World: The Epic Story of Dutch Manhattan and the Forgotten Colony That Shaped America*. New York: Vintage Books, 2005.

Tantillo, L. F. *The Edge of New Netherland*. Self-published Via CreateSpace, 2011.

Van der Donck, Adriaen. *Description of the New Netherlands*. New York: CosimoClassics, 2010.

From New Amsterdam to New York:
Dutch Settlement of America

Websites

New Amsterdam History Center

http://www.newamsterdamhistorycenter.org

For a 3D tour of drawings of New Amsterdam, visit this site.

New Netherland Institute

http://www.newnetherlandinstitute.org

Devoted to exploring Dutch heritage, this site offers links to articles, research, programs, and more.

NYC Department of Records & Information Services Records of New Amsterdam

http://www.archives.nyc/newamsterdam

For a glimpse of original maps and records from New Amsterdam, including Peter Stuyvesant's first edict, visit this site.

Bibliography

Books

Baskas, Richard S. *Cornelis Melyn: 3rd Patroon, Staten Island, New York*. Bloomington, IN: Xlibris. 2017.

Fabend, Firth Haring. *New Netherland in a Nutshell: A Concise History of the Dutch Colony in North America*. Albany, NY: New Netherland Institute, 2012.

Klein, Milton M., and New York State Historical Association. *The Empire State: A History of New York*. Ithaca, NY: Cornell University Press, 2001.

Shorto, Russell. *The Island at the Center of the World: The Epic Story of Dutch Manhattan and the Forgotten Colony That Shaped America*. New York: Vintage Books, 2005.

Van der Donck, Adriaen. *Description of the New Netherlands*. New York: CosimoClassics, 2010.

Online Articles

Benchley, Nathanial. "The $24 Swindle." American Heritage, December 1959. http://www.americanheritage.com/content/24-swindle.

"Cornelis Melyn." Nycourts.gov. Accessed March 31, 2017. http://www.nycourts.gov/history/legal-history-new-york/luminaries-dutch/melyn-cornelis.html.

Editors of Encyclopedia Britannica. "Peter Stuyvesant: Dutch Colonial Governor." Encyclopedia Britannica. Updated May 29, 2013. https://www.britannica.com/biography/Peter-Stuyvesant.

Jogues, Father Isaac. "Description (1643) of Nieuw Nederland (New York and Albany) from a Narrative of Father Isaac Jogues." August 3, 1646. Colonial Voyage. Accessed April 27, 2017. http://www.colonialvoyage.com/dutch-new-york.

Kenyon, John P. "James II: King of Great Britain." Encyclopedia Britannica, October 12, 2010. https://www.britannica.com/biography/James-II-king-of-Great-Britain.

"New Amsterdam Becomes New York." History.com. Accessed March 31, 2017. http://www.history.com/this-day-in-history/new-amsterdam-becomes-new-york.

Pricket, Abacuk. "Excerpt from 'A Larger Discourse of the Same Voyage.'" 1625. Computing in the Humanities and Social Sciences. Accessed March 23, 2017. http://homes.chass.utoronto.ca/~cpercy/hell/anthology/travel/Travel1625Pricket.htm.

Stone, Andrea. "New Online Archive Shows Colonial New York Was Rowdy, Filthy, Smelly." National Geographic, December 21, 2014. http://news.nationalgeographic.com/news/2014/12/141220-new-amsterdam-new-york-archives.

World Digital Library. "Freedoms, as Given by the Council of the Nineteen of the Chartered West India Company to All Those Who Want to Establish a Colony in New Netherland." Library of Congress. Updated September 22, 2014. https://www.wdl.org/en/item/4068.

Index

Page numbers in **boldface**
are illustrations. Entries in
boldface are glossary terms.

About the Author

Kate Shoup has written more than forty books and has edited hundreds more. When not working, Kate loves to travel, watch IndyCar racing, ski, read, and ride her motorcycle. She lives in Indianapolis with her husband, her daughter, and their dog. To learn more about Kate and her work, visit www.kateshoup.com.